INTRODUCTION

Deaf Culture 101: A Visual Reference to Deaf Culture, American Sign Language and ASL Interpreting is a photo book designed to give every student, teacher, interpreter, family member and professional an opportunity to learn about Deaf Culture, ASL and fields of interpreting as visually as possible.

Gilda Toby Ganezer is a Deaf ASL Professor and filmmaker from an all-Deaf family. Ms. Ganezer will be your narrator for over 55 illustrations seen throughout this book. These are based on Gilda's life experience, too.

This valuable photo book is designed best also for classroom use. Each and every page is conveniently and clearly divided into **three categories** as follows:

1 PHOTO / ILLUSTRATION

2 GILDA'S NARRATION

3 10 DISCUSSION QUESTIONS

All discussion questions are excellent for one-on-one conversations, group dialogues and even as homework / class assignments to further develop a clear understanding of what Deaf Culture is all about.

TABLE OF CONTENTS

Don't tell me to LIPREAD!

Can you tell the difference between:

I hate coffee
I hate coughing

I ate peas
I hate beets

My bat is dirty
My mat is dirty

So, please use ASL !

— GILDA TOBY GANEZER

Hello to everyone who understands ASL..
I have lost count as to how many times people would ask me this, "Can you read lips?", and I would typically respond, "Yes, every other day!"

It seems that lipreading is convenient to those who do not know ASL or are not willing to get an interpreter...

So, here is my quote for you to share with anyone.

In final words, I would rather give you a kiss with my lips than a lipreading lesson!

♡ Gilda

Discussion Questions

1. Which 5 words do you think are hard to lipread?

2. Is lipreading part of ASL?

3. How do you think Deaf people feel about lipreading?

4. How many percent is lipreading understood?

5. Is it rude to ask Deaf people if they lipread?

6. Why is lipreading not reliable?

7. Which 5 word pairs are about the same to lipread from?

8. How do you educate a hearing person about lipreading?

9. Why do some people try encouraging Deaf people to lipread?

10. Why is an ASL interpreter much more effective than lipreading?

"**Learning ASL without Deaf Culture is like eating French fries *without* ketchup.**"

- Gilda Toby Ganezer

Visit EverydayASL.com

©Everyday ASL Productions, Ltd.

Learning American Sign Language without Deaf Culture is like eating French fries without ketchup.

Deaf Culture and American Sign Language are truly connected and dependent upon one another.

Just like with any other languages that are enriched with culture.

XO Gilda

Discussion Questions

1. What is the difference between ASL and Deaf Culture?

2. What happens when you learn ASL without Deaf Culture?

3. Where can a person go to learn about Deaf Culture?

4. Can a Deaf person not know much about Deaf Culture? Why?

5. What are 3 good examples of Deaf Culture?

6. What is the difference between <u>d</u>eaf and <u>D</u>eaf?

7. Why is Deaf Culture important?

8. Why should ASL interpreters be familiar with Deaf Culture?

9. Should Deaf schools teach Deaf Culture? Why?

10. Who do you think should learn Deaf Culture?

One of the things I learned in life is to be TRUE to myself - especially when it comes to signing at public places.

People used to tell me to "calm down" whenever I show emotions via ASL which is one of my biggest pet peeve...

This is just to remind everyone to never tell a signer to... calm down.

Whenever we display emotions via ASL, we are actually giving others complete information of what we are trying to say.

Wink! Gilda

©Everyday ASL Productions, Ltd.

I CAN'T KEEP CALM I'M STILL SIGNING..

Discussion Questions

1. Why is it wrong to tell a Deaf person signing to "calm down"?

2. Why is showing emotions while signing important?

3. Should Deaf people sign with controlled emotions? Why not?

4. What information will be missing if no emotions are shown?

5. How will you educate hearing people about this?

6. Can hearing people show emotions while signing, too? Why?

7. If you are an ASL interpreter, how does emotions affect voicing?

8. If a hearing client tells a Deaf client to calm down signing, what would you do as an ASL interpreter?

9. If you see a parent tells their Deaf child to calm down whenever she or he is signing, what would you do?

10. Can you tell the difference between Deaf people signing with emotions and Deaf people yelling / screaming in ASL? How?

"Life without ASL is like a tree without blossoms or fruit."

Gilda Toby Ganezer

Visit EverydayASL.com

© Everyday ASL Productions, Ltd.

American Sign Language is truly a visual and gestural language.

ASL has its own semantic and syntactic structure, used by Deaf people in the United States, parts of Canada as well as the rest of the world.

Without ASL, there won't be any Deaf Culture, Deaf Community, ASL events, ASL poetry, ASL storytelling, ASL interpreters, and so on...

No ASL means no life for us all Deaf people.

Gilda

Discussion Questions

1. Is American Sign Language a written language? Why not?

2. Do people need to use voice when communicating in ASL?

3. Where do Deaf people learn ASL?

4. How is Signed English different from ASL?

5. About how long has ASL been used in the United States?

6. What does sign parameters mean for ASL? Name 3 parameters.

7. Do ASL signs stay the same over the years? Why or why not?

8. There are ASL or sign variations. What does that mean? Should you learn as many sign variations as possible? Why?

9. If you see someone using ASL incorrectly, what would you do? What kind of approach would you use to help?

10. What are the benefits of teaching ASL to Deaf children at an early age? How would this help them?

My *dog* knew I am *Deaf* because she would always get my attention with her paw.

At first, my dog would bark or whine to get my attention...but without success. It took little or no time for her to adapt by using her paw to get my attention. So smart, I would always reward her with a hug or a little milk-bone.

Lots of different animals will realize that Deaf people do not respond to sounds. In turn, these animals would use their paws and even faces or heads to get your attention adorably.

Please be kind to share this with anyone who has a pet.

♥ Gilda

Gilda Toby Ganezer

Discussion Questions

1. Have you ever seen a dog use paws to get attention? How?

2. What other animals do you think uses paws to get attention?

3. What do dogs do to get attention, other than using paws?

4. Can dogs understand ASL? What words would you teach?

5. What five (5) reasons do you think dogs' use of paws are for?

6. What about Deaf dogs? Do they still use paws to get attention?

7. Would you possibly adopt Deaf dogs or cats? Share your thoughts.

8. Could you use your hand to get Deaf dogs' attention? Show how you would call a Deaf dog without startling her/him.

9. What three (3) organizations and groups are available that provides shelter, adoption and support for Deaf pets?

10. Research and find a success story about adopting a Deaf dog. Share with pictures and explain how she/he was found, raised, etc.

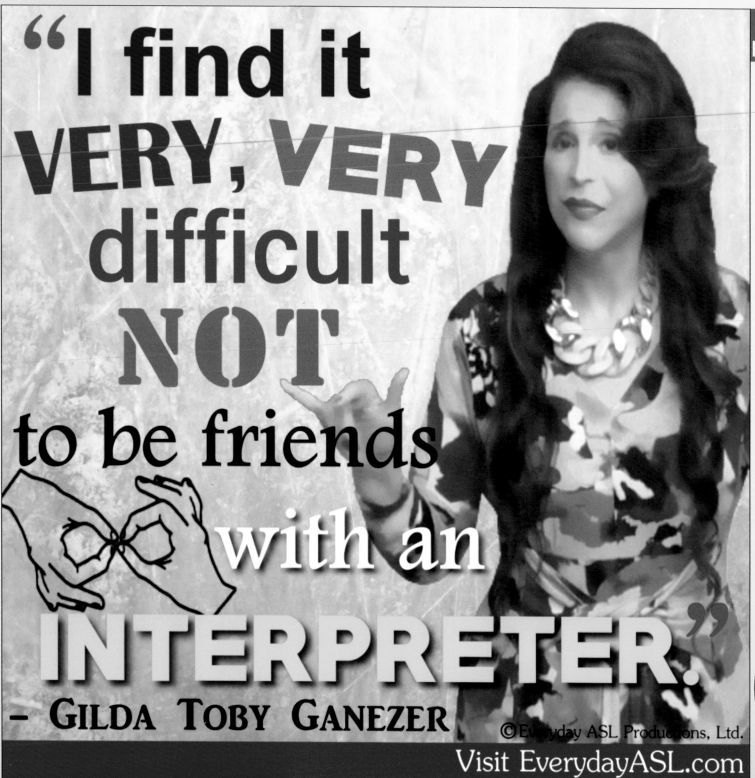

"I find it VERY, VERY difficult NOT to be friends with an INTERPRETER."

— GILDA TOBY GANEZER

©Everyday ASL Productions, Ltd.

Visit EverydayASL.com

This is exactly how I feel every time I work with an interpreter despite what code of ethics say these days..

"No strings attached" is technically non-existent in my world - in other words - not being friends with an interpreter is not easy because we share the same language and empowerment.

Sigh, all interpreters: I love you! Gilda

Discussion Questions

1. Why is it hard for Deaf people NOT to be friends with interpreters?

2. Should an interpreter avoid friendship with the Deaf client? Why?

3. How would a Deaf client feel when an interpreter "draws the line"?

4. Should an interpreter hug a Deaf client to say goodbye? Why not?

5. Can an interpreter befriend a Deaf client on Facebook? Why not?

6. If an interpreter or a Deaf client becomes intimate, what to do?

7. How can an interpreter respectfully set their boundaries?

8. What should be done if an interpreter bumps into a Deaf client at a grocery store after the assignment?

9. What should be done if an interpreter and Deaf client met 15 minutes too early prior to an assignment?

10. Once an interpreter and Deaf client become friends, should the interpreter give up the assignment to avoid conflict? Explain.

When I'm happy, I use ASL.

When I'm angry, I use Signed English.

When I'm confused, I use PSE.

So, I better always STAY HAPPY!!

- Gilda Toby Ganezer

This quote is what I would like to share with you.

You know, I grew up in a diverse environment where communication modes have always been changing for me.

So, aside from all my Freudian slips, I do still make plenty of communication slips whenever my emotions fluctuate.

Looks like I must always carry a chocolate treat to stay ASL.

Hugs, Gilda

Discussion Questions

1. What did Gilda mean? Explain.

2. What is American Sign Language? Explain.

3. What is Signed English? Explain.

4. What is PSE? What is it short for? Explain.

5. Show an example sentence that is PSE.

6. Why did Gilda say that she better always stay happy?

7. Can an interpreter also have fluctuating modes of communication?

8. If you see a Deaf person trying to apologize to you for changing modes of communication (not on purpose) while signing, what would you say or do?

9. Do you know what mode of communication some of your Deaf friends use? What do they use?

10. How does a person stick to using ASL? Explain.

I ♥ DEAF CHAT COFFEE

Deaf Culture

discuss politics

group selfies

share gossips

catch up news

ASL practice

Deaf & hearing dating

EverydayASL.com ©

CAUTION: THIS BEVERAGE IS EXTREMELY ASL.

— GILDA TOBY GANEZER

I love hot-steaming coffee! Starbucks and countless other coffee shops / cafes make best place for Deaf people and ASL lovers to meet up, socialize and chat - especially during the holiday season.

I would loooooove to see a coffee cup that looks like this picture! Maybe one day Starbucks and/or any other coffee shops are willing to print ASL on their cups!! This quote of mine is what Santa would approve.

Hope to bump into you for a cup of hazelnut coffee one day, who knows Gilda, forever.

Discussion Questions

1. What 3 reasons are coffee shops / cafes perfect for ASL users?

2. How often do you think the meet should be?

3. Where else are also perfect for the meet? Name 3 other places.

4. Should "no Spoken English" rule be enforced at the meet? Why?

5. Do you think these meets are typically brief or long? Explain.

6. How will you naturally blend into group ASL conversations?

7. If you don't understand a sign, what do you do?

8. What if the coffee shop staff does not know ASL for Deaf customers at time of ordering? What would you do to help?

9. If you notice other customers making fun of people using ASL, what would you do? Explain your approaches.

10. How will you know if Deaf people are interested in chatting with you? How do you determine their feelings while chatting?

If anyone says "You sign just like a Deaf person." Then it is a COMPLIMENT.

- Gilda Toby Ganezer

Whenever you see a hearing or Deaf person sign at any gathering, the way she/he signs can help others, including myself, get an impression (can tell) that this person is a native ASL user or anyone who signs like a "Deaf" person because of how much of the following are used:

- idioms in ASL
- facial expressions
- body movements
- fluency
- ASL classifiers
- complete ASL sentences

This list can go on and on. Sometimes people would say that a person who signs just like a Deaf person has a "DEAF ACCENT". If anyone who says you have a Deaf Accent or sign like a Deaf person, you should PAT YOURSELF on the back - that's a compliment! It also signifies your ASL ability and familiarity towards Deaf Culture! Sign like a Deaf person.. COME ON 🙂Gilda

Discussion Questions

1. What does a signer need to do to sign like a "Deaf" person?

2. How would you feel if someone says you have Deaf Accent?

3. Why do most CODAs (Children of Deaf Adults) have Deaf Accent?

4. If you do not sign like a "Deaf" person, why is that still okay?

5. Can a Deaf person using ASL still does not have an accent? Why?

6. Show 3 different idiomatic expressions in ASL.

7. Why is fluency important? Is fast better? Why not?

8. Do you know who signs with Deaf Accent? Who?

9. Why is it important to sign COMPLETE ASL sentences, rather than using 2-3 word sentences? Give an example.

10. ASL classifiers are a challenge for many but they help with the accent. Show 2 ASL classifier examples in one sentence.

> " I am Deaf. My speech will always sound funny to hearing people. But this does not give anyone the right to think low of me. "
>
> - Gilda Toby Ganezer

Don't you just hate it when other people look down on you. For example, when I was at a store and tried using my speech to say just one or two words (like "I APPRECIATE"), they immediately acted different / funny and looked at me with disappointment. That's audism...Actually, I am the one that should look at them with disappointment because they don't take the time to respect and/or learn my language and culture. Their lack of etiquette from ignorance really kills me. So, in the end, I was able to use my speech by saying "kiss my ass" just before I left the store - it was amazing how they suddenly understood me clearly!

Oh boy, really!

Just me,
Gilda Toby Ganezer

Discussion Questions

1. Like with countless other Deaf people, why was Gilda upset?

2. What 3 ideas do you have to resolve the situation described?

3. How should the hearing store staff behave in this situation?

4. How did Gilda know about hearing people's attitudes? Explain.

5. Which 10 ASL words do you think that every store should know?

6. Can a Deaf person ask for an interpreter at any stores? Explain.

7. What or how can Gilda do to report the incident? Where?

8. Can you define the word "audism"?

9. What are 3 good examples of audism today? Explain.

10. If you work at a store and saw that your co-worker, who does not know ASL, was having trouble communicating with a Deaf customer, what would you do to help? How?

If you do not know a sign for a word, do **NOT** be afraid to fingerspell it.

p.s. Fingerspelling a word does not mean you don't know ASL!

– Gilda Toby Ganezer

You have no idea how many times a hearing person would voice a "big" word and my interpreter would swallow a bit hard and then fingerspell like a pro. I would feel uncomfortable whenever anyone makes up a sign for a "big" word to avoid fingerspelling. If you fingerspell a word, it does NOT mean you are not good in ASL, you are actually doing the right job! There are THOUSANDS of words that do not have signs for them so fingerspelling is important and necessary. True, you can translate a "big" word with a sign of similar or same meaning BUT, sometimes, you need to FINGERSPELL the word, no buts about it. Also it is important for an interpreter to be familiar with the topic prior to accepting an assignment so s/he won't have to worry about misspellings. And, anyway, please fingerspell my name right, please. I won't tell you my name.

Discussion Questions

1. Is it okay to make up a sign instead of fingerspelling it? Explain.

2. Give 5 word examples that must be fingerspelled.

3. What tips do you have to fingerspell fluently?

4. If you fingerspell a lot, does it mean you don't know ASL?

5. If you misspell a word, how do you self-correct while interpreting?

6. How can you EMPHASIZE a fingerspelled word? Explain.

7. How helpful will fingerspelled words be for Deaf clients?

8. As an interpreter, if you do not know how to fingerspell a word, what do you do?

9. Think of 3 medication names that you will need to fingerspell. (i.e. synthroid, crestor, nexium, etc.) Be fluent!

10. Think of 4 "big" last names that you will need to fingerspell. (i.e. Abernathy, Gallagher, Richardson, Worthington, etc.)

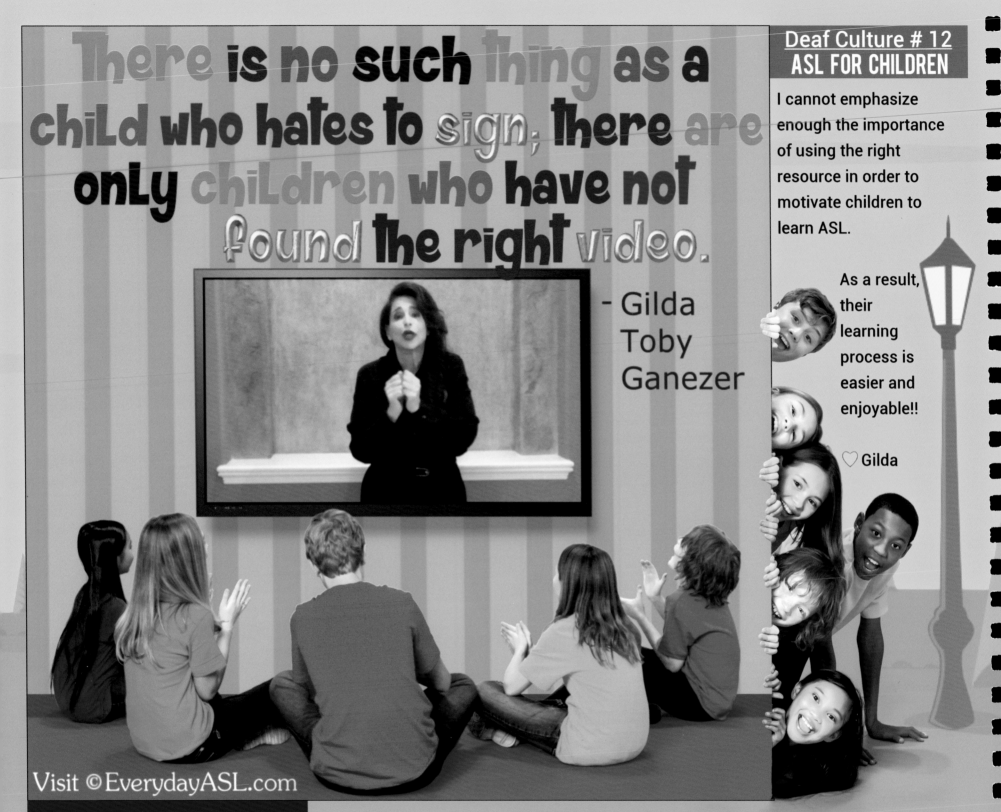

There is no such thing as a child who hates to sign; there are only children who have not found the right video.

— Gilda Toby Ganezer

I cannot emphasize enough the importance of using the right resource in order to motivate children to learn ASL.

As a result, their learning process is easier and enjoyable!!

♡ Gilda

Visit © EverydayASL.com

Discussion Questions

1. How early do you think babies can start learning ASL?

2. Make a list of 20 best words to start teaching babies.

3. How do you know if an ASL video for kids are enjoyable?

4. Should materials be the same to teach Deaf and hearing kids?

5. Should parents watch ASL videos along with children? Why?

6. Name 3 websites online that are best for kids to learn ASL from.

7. What will you review what kids learned on video? Explain.

8. Which games or toys do you think that will promote ASL education among children? Name several examples.

9. How will you review the ASL words and sentences that a child learned from the videos? Share your ideas.

10. Where can kids go to learn ASL other than watching ASL videos? Name 3 places that kids can go to get themselves exposed to ASL.

An experienced **ASL** interpreter was once a beginner **ASL STUDENT**

- Gilda Toby Ganezer

Like with every profession, every master was once a beginner. So, for any of you with aspirations to do anything should always be reminded that you will make it all the way to the top, too!

You can do it, trust me!!

♡ Gilda

Discussion Questions

1. How does this quote make you feel? Encouraged? Explain.

2. Name 5 ways an interpreter can do to practice their skills.

3. Are certified interpreters still learning? Why?

4. Why is it important for interpreters to view many ASL vlogs?

5. What kind of national interpreter certifications are out there?

6. What is a Deaf interpreter? Why do we really need them?

7. What part of interpreting test do you feel nervous about? Why?

8. If a Deaf client corrects an interpreter with the way she or he signs (word, idiom, etc.), what should the interpreter do?

9. If you were to start an interpreter training program, which 2 courses do you feel are most important to train? Why?

10. How do you feel about interpreter mentoring? What three benefits would mentoring do to prospective interpreters?

I HUG DEAF PEOPLE

→ DO YOU?

In the Deaf Community, we usually say

HELLO and GOODBYE with **HUGS** NOT handshakes!

— Gilda Toby Ganezer

I am Deaf.

I do not normally shake hands but almost always hug Deaf people when I say hello and/or goodbye. I even hug hearing people, too.

Deaf people normally greet one another with a hug as a cultural part of their deepest appreciation to finally see one another... Deaf world is "small".

So, when you see me, do expect a hug from me only if you are nice (arms-folding).

Kisses, Gilda

Discussion Questions

1. Have you ever seen Deaf people hug each other goodbye?

2. Can an interpreter hug a Deaf client at end of job? Why not?

3. Do you ask for permission before you hug? Explain why not.

4. Sometimes people do not want to be hugged, so what to do?

5. Show how you would greet with a hug. How does it feel?

6. What other ways can you use to say goodbye? (hint: ILY)

7. Is it wrong if you prefer to shake hands? What may happen?

8. How do you explain to hearing people who do not know Deaf Culture about hugging?

9. Do Deaf people of different nationalities still hug? Why or why not?

10. "SEE YOU LATER", "STAY-IN-TOUCH", etc. What 3 other goodbye ASL sentences can you think of?

"Like with any language, the way you sign can tell others who you really are."

— gilda Toby ganezer

As a lifelong ASL user, I am sharing my quote and this is not about signing skills - this is about recognizing people's character / personality based on the way she/he signs.

The way a person signs can tell you if she/he is friendly, warm, honest, aggressive, outspoken, conservative and even narcissistic.

Love to you all always,
Gilda

Visit EverydayASL.com

Discussion Questions

1. What does the quote really mean? Explain.

2. Show how to sign like a person who is friendly.

3. Show how to sign like a person who is narcissistic.

4. Show how to sign like a person who is soft-spoken.

5. Show how to sign like a person who is forceful.

6. Emotions do affect how you sign. Show several examples.

7. When you sign, can you tell how others are affected by you? How?

8. When you interpret, should you match hearing person's personality, too? Why or why not?

9. Sign the sentence: "I want more cookies." with three different personalities. Explain how you changed the way you sign.

10. When Deaf people sign slowly and clearly for some hearing people, what does that tell you about who Deaf people are?

"Never tell DEAF people to PICK UP THEIR FEET when they walk."

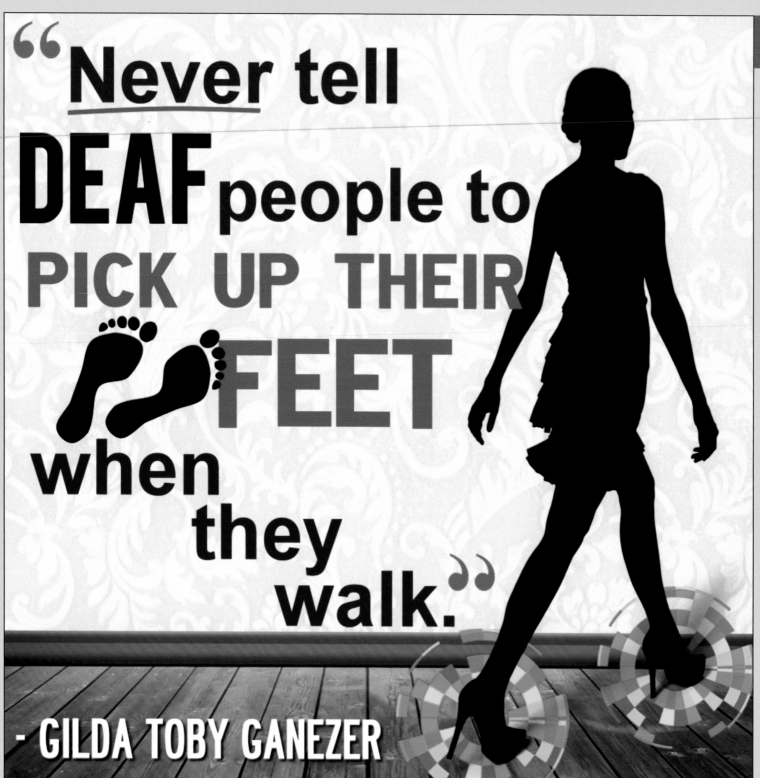

- GILDA TOBY GANEZER

Just because hearing people can hear, some of them feel "entitled" and play "parental" role by telling me how to behave throughout my life. Examples include: "lower your voice", "don't sign too big in public", "don't sign with food in your mouth" and especially one of my biggest pet peeves: "would you pick up your feet, you are walking like a dinosaur". Whoever said to me like that should have soap in their mouth!

Deaf people do not like being told how to behave just because they make some noise for others unintentionally.

Don't worry my friends, I am not going to let them control me, not anymore. When I put on my heel shoes, I will be sure the whole town could hear and feel me strut.

Whatever..Gilda

Discussion Questions

1. What three examples did Gilda say that she was told to behave?

2. Why do some hearing people feel "entitled" over the Deaf?

3. Do hearing people make natural noises, too? Like what?

4. Add 2 more examples of how Deaf people are told to behave?

5. Why is it wrong to tell Deaf people how to behave? Explain.

6. How do you educate others about being respectful? Explain.

7. Where do you think Deaf people tend to get told how to behave?

8. If you see an interpreter telling a Deaf client how to behave, how would you approach the interpreter and educate her / him?

9. You are at a library with Deaf and hearing friends. A librarian tells one of your Deaf friends not to sign too big, what do you do?

10. As an interpreter at a class, a hearing teacher tells a Deaf student to pick up his feet walking. What do you do?

Deaf people cannot work alone.

Hearing people cannot work alone.

Deaf and hearing people cannot work separately.

Unity is the only way.

- Gilda Toby Ganezer

UNITY is possible when Deaf and hearing people interact, exchange notes to work together anywhere, from Christmas parties to schools, so that Deaf Community can get a strong support during difficult times. Deaf people cannot work alone. Hearing people cannot work alone. Deaf and hearing people cannot work separately. Unity is the only way.

Several ingredients to successful relations are compassion, tolerance, understanding and and especially respect. Here is a tip for hearing friends and colleagues: Always open your ears, eyes, hearts and souls to the "voices" of the Deaf Community. Don't feel or decide for them, they can do that themselves. Don't be afraid, resistant or stubborn but to let them show you the way how to make things work.

Let all of us play UNO for unity's sake! 😉 Gilda

Discussion Questions

1. Explain what Gilda said about how unity can be achieved.

2. What happens when Deaf and hearing people work separately?

3. What are the 4 ingredients to successful relations?

4. What is Gilda's tip for hearing friends and colleagues?

5. What happens to the Deaf Community when unity is not formed?

6. Why do Deaf people sometimes work alone?

7. Why do hearing people sometimes work alone?

8. What three ideas do you have that promotes interaction between the Deaf and hearing peers? Explain your ideas.

9. Why is "Always open your ears, eyes, hearts and souls to the "voices" of the Deaf Community." important?

10. What is UNO card game? How do Deaf people play the game slightly different from how hearing people would?

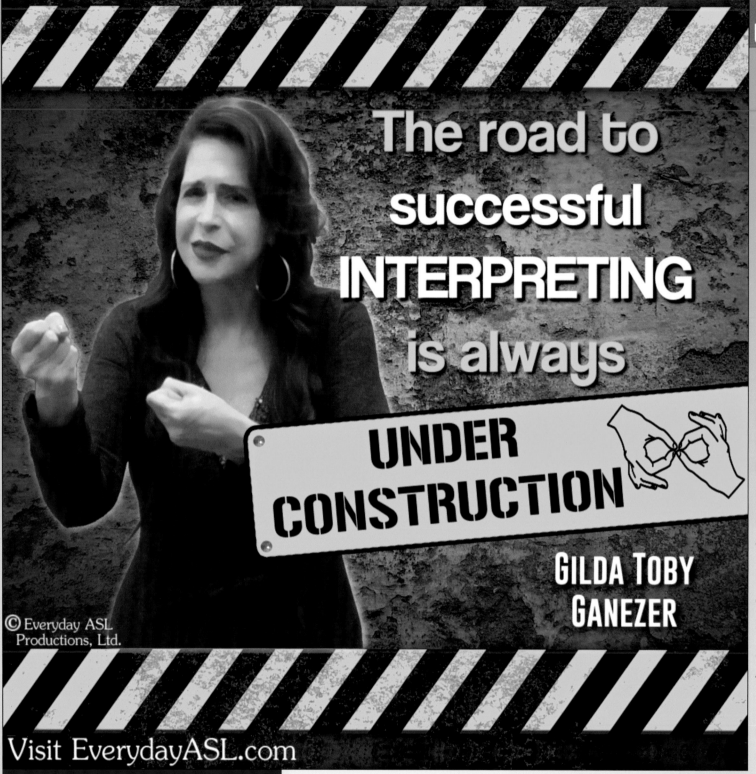

The road to successful INTERPRETING is always

UNDER CONSTRUCTION

GILDA TOBY GANEZER

© Everyday ASL Productions, Ltd.

Visit EverydayASL.com

As Deaf interpreter and educator myself, learning experience never ends for any and all interpreters, no matter what.

Even with the certified and qualified interpreters.

There are workshops, courses, trainings, conferences and adult education programs that are readily available for experienced interpreters to upkeep with words, idiomatic expressions, complex sentences, interpreting techniques, and issues related to the fields of interpreting.

Keep on interpreting!
♡ Gilda

Discussion Questions

1. Explain what Gilda said means for all interpreters?

2. Where do students / interpreters go to learn more?

3. If an interpreter is certified, then no more training? Why not?

4. What 5 workshop examples are best for interpreters to upkeep?

5. What area of interpreting do you feel is most challenging? Why?

6. Which 3 school subjects do you feel are most challenging? Why?

7. Make a list of 6 different interpreting assignments. (i.e.: court)

8. If an interpreter tells others that she / he is always learning and improving, why is that attitude positive? What does that show?

9. When an interpreter is done with an assignment with a Deaf client, how will the interpreter know if all went well?

10. How do interpreters learn and understand more about Deaf Culture? Where do interpreters go to learn more about it?

I and my heart love animals and I know you feel exactly the same. This goes the very same way for animals who are deaf.

Communication is so important, especially with Deaf animals who also have feelings and needs.

So, here's my quote for you.

Hugs, Gilda

"We do not always understand what Deaf animals are communicating... but their eyes are the mirror of their soul..."

- Gilda Toby Ganezer

Discussion Questions

1. What does Gilda mean with her quote? Explain.

2. Can ALL animals with ears become deaf? How?

3. How can you tell a deaf dog or cat understands you?

4. Can you teach several ASL words to a deaf dog or cat? How?

5. Who was Washoe? How many ASL words did she know?

6. Explain about Koko, a female gorilla and her knowledge of ASL.

7. Why do Deaf people work well with deaf dogs? Explain.

8. What happens to deaf dog's use of their other senses, including sight, smell and touch? Explain with examples.

9. Deaf pets may be startled more easily with strong vibrations. Are Deaf people like that, just as well? Explain why.

10. What 5 organizations are there that can help you add a deaf pet to your family? Explain a bit about each organization.

Do you know that all Deaf people are human beings? This means every Deaf person has feelings. One of my TRUE+BUSINESS (that means "really really" in English) pet peeves is whenever I am at a party, work, family gathering or a public place where there are some hearing people talking with one another (they DEFINITELY don't know ASL) and I would always ask around to see what they were saying and I get brushed off with these responses:

"I'll tell you later..."
"Oh, it's nothing!"
"It is not important."
"Never mind."
EVEN if some who know NO ASL still do not even try writing down on paper or talking slowly for me to force myself lipreading (UGH!!!) so I could understand because I know I cannot expect family gathering or party to hire an interpreter... But! Imagine, still, some know signs very well, they just do not feel like translating / interpreting almost at all.. WHY??!! (sigh - hands down in disgust) Well, point is?? It is because of some of their lack of patience, consideration and/or sensitivity. I know, it is "no fun" for hearing people to try writing on paper or translating, but trust me, it is NO fun for me being LEFT OUT!!

Just saying! Gilda
(I'm spraying perfume on my neck now...)

ASL GLOSS:
"THINK ME NOTHING"

English Translation:
"Think nothing of me."

Discussion Questions

1. What does this quote mean? Explain.

2. Why does this situation frustrates Deaf people so much?

3. What three common phrases do hearing people say?

4. What 3 reasons are there for hearing people's actions?

5. What does "THINK ME NOTHING" in ASL mean?

6. What 3 ideas do you have that would solve the problem?

7. Is hearing people's action a form of audism? Explain.

8. If you are the only Deaf person in an all hearing family, how would you explain to avoid a problem?

9. Why is it important that hearing people should also empower and help with this awareness? Explain.

10. What will happen if a Deaf person is always informed and included in group conversations by hearing peers?

A long time ago in a Deaf school far, far away... American Sign Language and Deaf Culture were hugely overlooked and oppressed. I have come a long, long way to being proud of my language and roots. Long time ago, there were no interpreters, video relay services, captioning and many other services for the Deaf. Yes, we have so much today, Thank God, but the battle for our rights and language / cultural preservation is still ongoing. Nobody likes any battles, really, but this fight must be made to keep ASL and Deaf Culture alive for future generations.

Thank you for your great support. It means a lot to me and the whole Deaf Community. Oh, anyway, for my quote - I am certainly a fan of Star Wars.

May the ASL be with you.
♥ Gilda

© GILDA TOBY GANEZER / EVERYDAYASL.COM

Discussion Questions

1. What was Gilda's explanation about? Explain.

2. What two most important things that were severely oppressed?

3. What two things did Gilda say that she was proud of?

4. What 6 services for the Deaf were nonexistent 100 years ago?

5. How can anyone fight to preserve ASL and Deaf Culture? Explain.

6. Identify who you see in the picture. What do each of them do?

7. Today, do you know of any oppressions of ASL? Where? Explain.

8. If some people from Earth moved to Mars, which sign language will be brought to that world? Why? How do people decide?

9. Like with 'Close Encounters of the Third Kind' movie, how do you think humans and aliens would communicate? Explain.

10. Let's imagine: If you became a superintendent of a Deaf school that has a policy that supports simultaneous communication (SimCom), what would you do? What changes will you make?

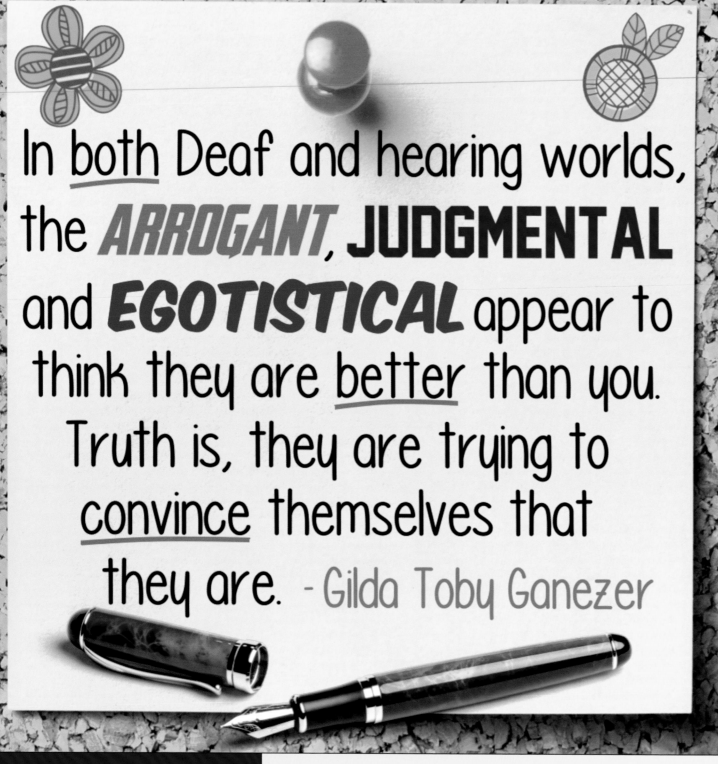

In both Deaf and hearing worlds, the *ARROGANT*, **JUDGMENTAL** and *EGOTISTICAL* appear to think they are better than you. Truth is, they are trying to convince themselves that they are. - Gilda Toby Ganezer

When I was a little girl, I grew up in a loving care-free home. My parents made sure I felt good about myself and my passion was to share my love and caring with other people. All that was shattered once I stepped into a Deaf school for the first time at age of 6. I remembered vividly being so beautifully dressed by my mom in a white dress for the first day of school. Sadly, I came home with my dress all ripped up and soiled simply because other children were insecure of how I dressed along with my friendly personality just because I wanted to talk to as many people as my heart desired – some students and even teachers immediately didn't like me for who I am. After years of growing up in that kind of environment and being exposed to outside world, meeting people of different cultures and backgrounds, I came to learn and truly understand the essence of how insecurities and jealousies of others can make them ARROGANT, JUDGMENTAL and EGOTISTICAL towards others.

So, my friends, let us all be strong, BELIEVE in ourselves and not let other people with insecurity problems control our lives. So, stay close with others who treat you with respect and appreciates you.

 Gilda

Discussion Questions

1. What happened to Gilda when she was a little girl? Explain.

2. How was Gilda able to share her love and care with others?

3. What were the reasons why children were insecure of Gilda?

4. Could teachers also be insecure of others? Explain.

5. How did Gilda learn about other people's insecurities?

6. How do you sign: "arrogant", "judgmental" and "egotistical"?

7. How can you tell if a Deaf person is being arrogant? Explain with an example.

8. How can you tell if a Deaf person is being judgmental? Explain with an example.

9. How can you tell if a Deaf person is being egotistical? Explain with an example.

10. Explain how you would help others, both Deaf and hearing, how to believe in themselves?

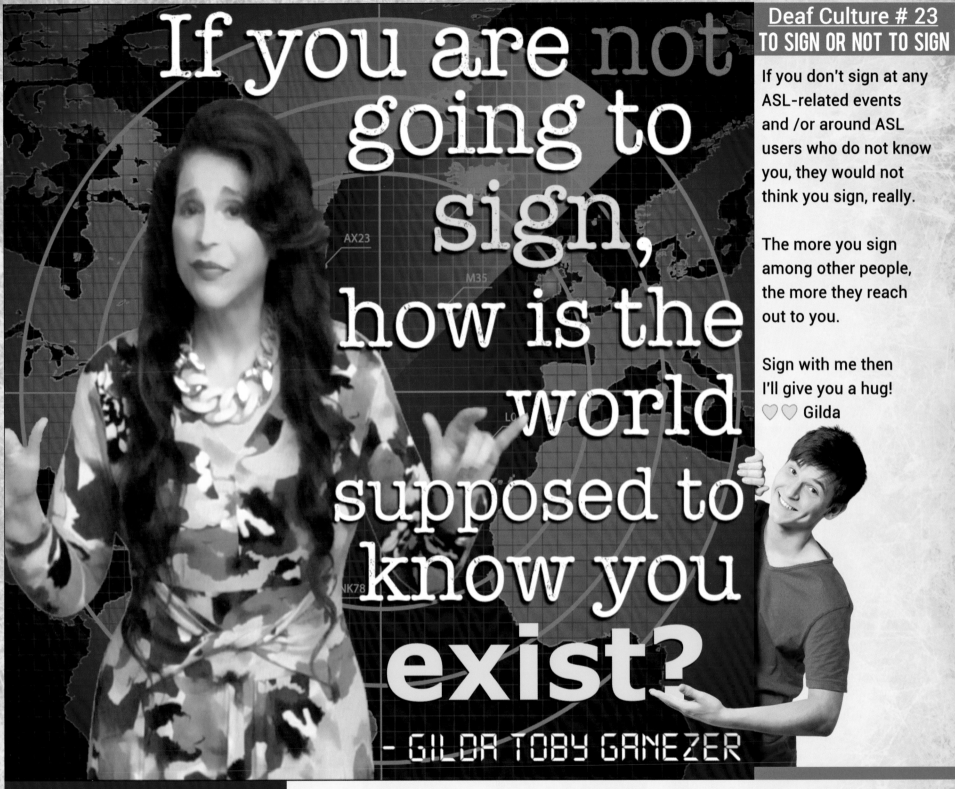

If you are not going to sign, how is the world supposed to know you exist?

— GILDA TOBY GANEZER

If you don't sign at any ASL-related events and /or around ASL users who do not know you, they would not think you sign, really.

The more you sign among other people, the more they reach out to you.

Sign with me then I'll give you a hug! ♡♡ Gilda

Discussion Questions

1. What does Gilda mean with the quote above? Explain.

2. Give 4 reasons why some people don't sign in public.

3. Give 4 examples of a large ASL-related event.

4. If you want to practice signing, where would you go?

5. What 3 topics do you think would promote ASL conversations?

6. Show how you would introduce yourself in ASL.

7. What do you do if you see someone who is shy in public?

8. If you see a Deaf person you know in public, how do you approach her / him? Demonstrate how you would do that.

9. What would you do to entertain a Deaf company? Share a Deaf / ASL-related joke. (Deaf people dig them)

10. When a person signs, it is important to give feedback WHILE she / he signs. Give 4 examples (i.e.: OH-I-SEE, REALLY?)

The Certification Committee certifies that

John Doe

has satisfied all the requirements and is duly licensed as an *ASL Interpreter*

December 26, 2015

Michael Smith
Chair

Michaela Smith
Secretary

CUSTOMER SATISFACTION
100%
GUARANTEED
★ ★ ★

WHATEVER INTERPRETER SERVICE
ESTABLISHED 2015
©EverydayASL.com

I appreciate if you are CERTIFIED to interpret!
But, TRUTHFULLY, I care if you are QUALIFIED to interpret!

– Gilda Toby Ganezer

I appreciate interpreters who are certified to interpret. Like with doctors, lawyers, and countless other professions, they all have gone through certain training and testing to get themselves certified or licensed. But...I had been unlucky working with some certified interpreters because of their level of qualification for a certain assignment. Here is an example: When I attended a conference for women as victims of Domestic Violence, a certified interpreter was provided and was unsuccessful in interpreting because of a number of words and phrases that she was not familiar with. It is important to note that a certified interpreter does not mean she or he is qualified to interpret at all situations. A qualified interpreter is encouraged to be certified PLUS have some life experience, be familiar with the topic / assignment, be immersed in Deaf Community and be open to criticism and feedback especially from Deaf clients (show good attitude than to be defensive).

It is VERY important that all certified interpreters are honest about their qualification to do the job.

My point: I like certified interpreters but I like qualified interpreters BEST.

Gilda

Discussion Questions

1. What is a certified interpreter? Which agencies?

2. Why is a certified interpreter not qualified for all jobs?

3. How can an interpreter be qualified? Explain.

4. What did Gilda mean by showing a good attitude?

5. How can an interpreter be more familiar with a topic/job?

6. How can an interpreter be immersed in Deaf Community?

7. If you feel you are not qualified to interpret an assignment, what do you do?

8. If you are to interpret for a Deaf client in court and she / he does not understand you too well, what do you do?

9. What do you do if an interpreter service agency hires you to do an assignment BUT you realize you are not qualified? Explain.

10. How will an interpreter know she / he did well interpreting? What does she / he look for?

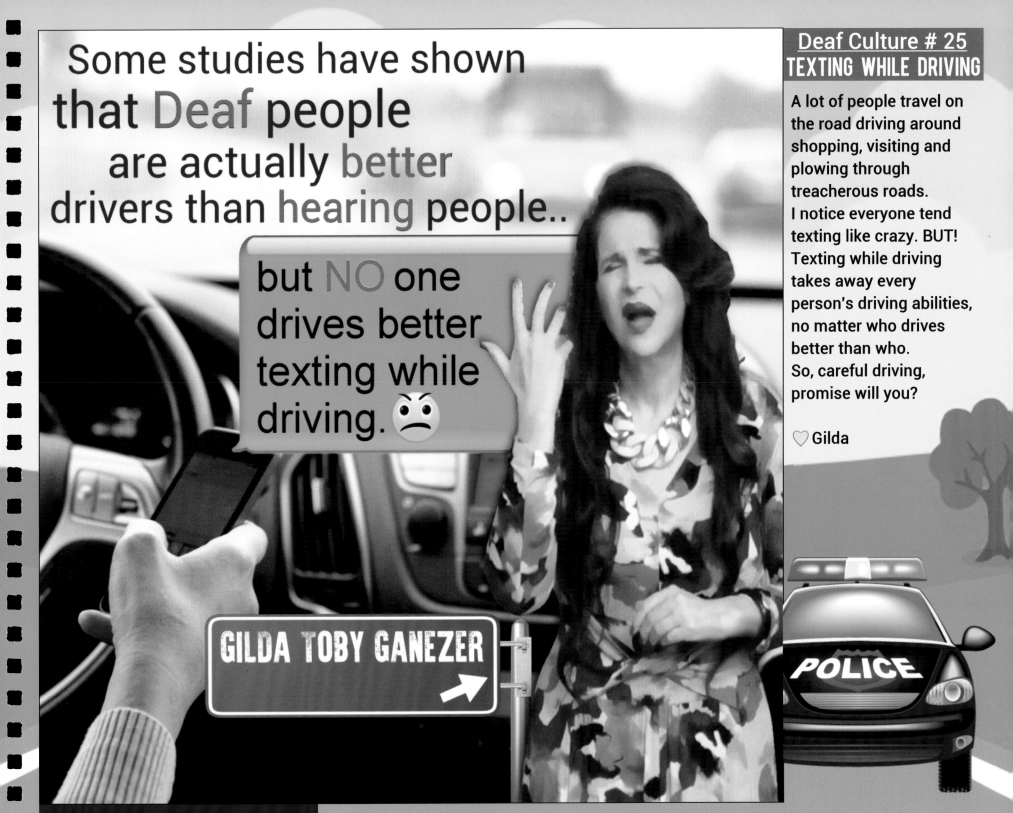

A lot of people travel on the road driving around shopping, visiting and plowing through treacherous roads. I notice everyone tend texting like crazy. BUT! Texting while driving takes away every person's driving abilities, no matter who drives better than who. So, careful driving, promise will you?

♡ Gilda

Discussion Questions

1. Explain why some Deaf people drive better than hearing.

2. What should Deaf and hearing person do about the issue?

3. What laws are in effect about texting while driving? Explain.

4. Do all police know ASL? Why or why not?

5. Make a list of 10 ASL words every police should know.

6. Should every police learn basic Deaf Culture? Explain.

7. Some Deaf people have handicapped parking permit. Why?

8. If a cop pulls over a Deaf driver for texting while driving, how should the Deaf person identify her / his disability?

9. Should every EMT and firefighter know ASL? If so, what 5 ASL words or basic sentences should they learn?

10. If a crime occurs and a Deaf person needs to be handcuffed, should it be in front of body or behind the back? Explain.

This Thanksgiving, please do not be **AFRAID** to bring **A S L** to the dinner table.

— Gilda Toby Ganezer

Happy Thanksgiving!

Thanksgiving is when most families and friends gather to catch up on all the things in life.

Please make sure ASL is being used especially at the dinner table so NO one would be left out.

So, here is my quote and I wish every one of you the most safe and happiest Thanksgiving!

Again, I really wish I could give you a hug BECAUSE I am thankful. Gilda

MENU
- PATIENCE
- ASL
- DEAF JOKES
- PAPER & PEN
- SHARING

Discussion Questions

1. What did Gilda mean in the picture? Explain.

2. If a Deaf guest is at the dinner table, what will you do to help?

3. How will you guide other families with this situation? Explain.

4. What 4 family events should be interpreted? (i.e. wedding)

5. How would a Deaf person feel being left out at a dinner table?

6. What first 10 ASL words / phrases should a hearing family learn?

7. Deaf people love Deaf jokes. Share a Deaf joke in ASL.

8. If a hearing family member insists that a Deaf person uses speech instead of signing at the dinner table, what would you do?

9. If a family dinner is at a restaurant, what would you do to be sure that Deaf guests are included without being left out? (hint: servers)

10. What about cafeterias during lunch? How will a Deaf student not be left out from other students at a public school? Explain.

"What if the KID you bullied at school, grew up, and turned out to be the only qualified INTERPRETER who could save your life?"

~ Gilda Toby Ganezer

©Everyday ASL Productions, Ltd.

Visit EverydayASL.com

As you may know, throughout the Deaf Community, the fight against bullying is ongoing, but through the promotion of positivity and clear communication.

Let us all work together to create a Bully Free world for every individual..

♡ Gilda

Discussion Questions

1. What did Gilda mean with the quote? Explain.

2. Do bullying exist within Deaf Community? Explain.

3. How will you know if a Deaf child is bullied?

4. How do ASL interpreters get bullied? Give 3 examples.

5. What 4 kinds of bullying are there?

6. Name 3 organizations that offer services to Deaf victims of bullying.

7. What should you do if your Deaf child is being bullied?

8. What should you do if your Deaf child is being cyberbullied?

9. What if you know about another Deaf child who is being bullied?

10. What if your Deaf child is bullying other children?

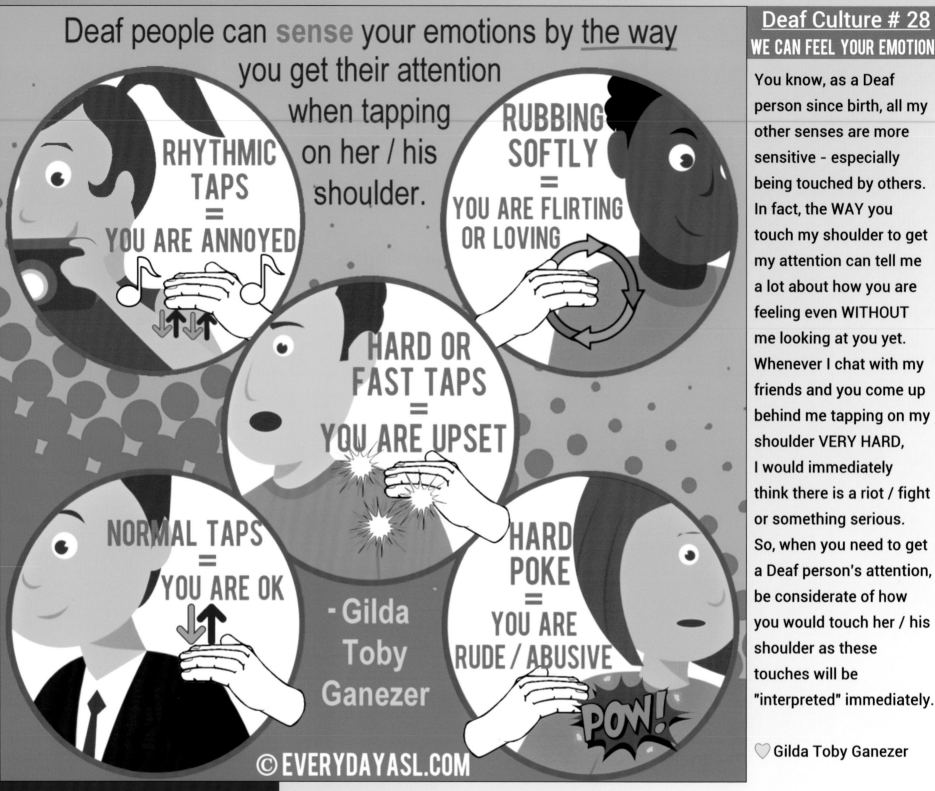

Deaf people can sense your emotions by the way you get their attention when tapping on her / his shoulder.

RHYTHMIC TAPS = YOU ARE ANNOYED

RUBBING SOFTLY = YOU ARE FLIRTING OR LOVING

HARD OR FAST TAPS = YOU ARE UPSET

NORMAL TAPS = YOU ARE OK

HARD POKE = YOU ARE RUDE / ABUSIVE

POW!

- Gilda Toby Ganezer

© EVERYDAYASL.COM

You know, as a Deaf person since birth, all my other senses are more sensitive - especially being touched by others. In fact, the WAY you touch my shoulder to get my attention can tell me a lot about how you are feeling even WITHOUT me looking at you yet. Whenever I chat with my friends and you come up behind me tapping on my shoulder VERY HARD, I would immediately think there is a riot / fight or something serious. So, when you need to get a Deaf person's attention, be considerate of how you would touch her / his shoulder as these touches will be "interpreted" immediately.

♡ Gilda Toby Ganezer

Discussion Questions

1. What is Gilda's main point about what Deaf people can sense?

2. If rhythmic taps were felt on the shoulder, what does it mean?

3. If hard/fast taps were felt on the shoulder, what does it mean?

4. If normal taps were felt on the shoulder, what does it mean?

5. If soft rubbing were felt on the shoulder, what does it mean?

6. If a hard poke was felt on the shoulder, what does it mean?

7. Explain how you would educate hearing people about these taps.

8. If the Deaf person you want to get attention from is across the room, what 3 ways would you use to properly get attention?

9. If you see a hearing person tapping on the back of a Deaf person's head, which is a NO-NO, what do you do?

10. Is it acceptable to tug or even use objects (like a branch or a ruler) to get a Deaf person's attention? Explain.

To be a >>> successful ASL teacher, you need to FALL IN LOVE with ASL first. <<<

— Gilda Toby Ganezer

There is a motto, "do what you do best" - it is also imperative to do it with true passion and love right from the heart.

This is why I admire each and every ASL teacher for their devotion and hard work.

Have a blessed day,
Gilda

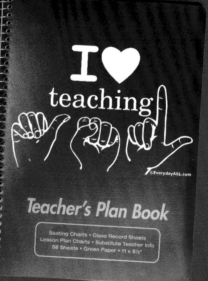

I ♥ teaching

Teacher's Plan Book

Seating Charts • Class Record Sheets
Lesson Plan Charts • Substitute Teacher Info
50 Sheets • Green Paper • 11 x 8½"

©EverydayASL.com

Discussion Questions

1. What does Gilda's quote mean? Explain.

2. How different will it be to teach WITHOUT love for ASL?

3. How do one become an ASL teacher? Explain

4. Can an ASL teacher teach without certification? Explain.

5. Which curriculum do you think is best for ASL teachers today?

6. Why is ASL grammar so important? What is it, generally?

7. Why are ASL sentence structures important to teach? Explain.

8. Can a person, also a native ASL user, automatically be an ASL teacher without teacher training? Why or why not?

9. When you teach ASL, should you use spoken English (voices) to help with teaching? Why or why not?

10. If you are an ASL teacher at a local high school and you get to choose a class field trip to enrichen ASL and Deaf Culture, what place would be your top choice? Explain why.

Domestic violence speaks in all languages including American Sign Language.

REPORT IT. STOP IT IN ASL!

– GILDA TOBY GANEZER

It is the hardest thing for me to do, simply because I was a victim of domestic violence throughout my life. As a Deaf woman, I had such difficulties opening up about being abused by others, especially when there are little or no organizations for Deaf individuals of domestic and sexual violence. As time goes by, public awareness, new laws and ongoing activism has made me feel stronger and given me the ability to open up all because I want to be healed. I want other individuals to get help and heal, just as well... Yes, domestic violence do exist within a Deaf family and their peers. There are help out there, thank God. DeafHope (http://www.deaf-hope.org) is an excellent example where every individual can go to for support. You, my dear friends and new friends, can make a difference. Do not be afraid to report it. Do not be afraid to stop it. There are lots of help out there for you. Because it is time for you to heal, you deserve it. Life is too precious to pass up so be strong and unite with others so the violence will gradually stop.

Thinking of you and others!
Gilda

Discussion Questions

1. What did Gilda say about domestic violence? Explain.

2. Why was it hard for Gilda to open up about being abused?

3. What made Gilda feel stronger about taking action?

4. Can domestic violence exist within a Deaf family? Explain.

5. What is DeafHope? What does it do and who is it for?

6. What are two actions Gilda said not to be afraid of?

7. Are there other Deaf organizations like DeafHope? Explain.

8. There are five forms of domestic violence: Physical, sexual, psychological, emotional and economic. Give 2 examples of each.

9. What 20 words / short sentences in ASL would you teach the staff at a local battered women shelter to prepare ahead of time?

10. What would you do to raise awareness in your community about domestic violence towards Deaf individuals? Explain 3 ways.

Mixing ASL and *oralism* is like trying to mix OIL and water

- Gilda Toby Ganezer -

Me curious.. When you combine oil and water in a glass cup then stir it with a spoon for a couple of minutes, what happens to the solution? Can both oil and water be mixed together permanently? What happens to the solution after an hour? Of course oil and water CANNOT mix together! Really amazing. So, some things CANNOT be mixed or combined. ASL is a language that has it own SYNTAX, FACIAL EXPRESSIONS, BODY MOVEMENT and MOUTH MOVEMENT that cannot be mixed or combined with oralism and/or other communication "modes". No, you cannot negotiate or compromise with ASL. Whoever tries to breakdown ASL is no different from trying to breakdown English or any other languages. Once you take away a feature that is required for ASL to be a language, it no longer is considered ASL, I repeat, it no longer is a language.

Mixing ASL and oralism is like trying to mix oil and water. Simple.

Wink, Gilda

Discussion Questions

1. What did Gilda mean? Explain.

2. What happens to ASL when you mix with oralism?

3. What exactly does oralism mean? Explain.

4. What is simultaneous communication? Explain.

5. Why do some Deaf people appear to be oralists?

6. How do you think some Deaf people think of oralism?

7. Is it true that ASL is considered a language? Explain why.

8. Do you think a Deaf child should learn how to use speech? Why or why not? Explain your thoughts.

9. How would a Deaf person feel if a hearing person tries to correct her/his speech? Explain several possible reactions.

10. What is a Bilingual–Bicultural Deaf education program? What are the benefits? Explain.

A good friend who knows **A S L**, is like a 4-LEAF CLOVER: hard to find & LUCKY to have!

To every friend, best friend and very best friend,

This is my 32nd quote. No matter how many ASL classes are out there. No matter how many ASL DVDs we sell throughout the world. No matter how many schools teach ASL courses. There will always, always be so many people that do not know even how to fingerspell a word. Whenever I see anyone sign a simple sentence in ASL to me in public (waitress, police, neighbor, etc.) my heart will start pacing with joy as I say to myself "YES!!!! Sign with me, sign with me!!!" Believe me, I am still an ordinary Deaf girl who appreciates anyone signing with me anywhere - a good friend with ASL knowledge is still so hard to find.

So, if any of you know ASL, then you are my 4-leaf clover for life and I would give you a kiss for life.

Happy St. Patrick's Day,

Gilda 🖤

Discussion Questions

1. What did Gilda mean? Explain.

2. Should every police officer know ASL? Why?

3. Should every firefighter know ASL? Why?

4. Should every doctor know ASL? Why?

5. What 5 simple ASL sentences should be taught?

6. Which 10 ASL words are most important?

7. Is fingerspelling important? Why?

8. Should EVERY family member of a Deaf relative know ASL? Why?

9. If you see a Deaf person you do not know at a public place, would you go and say hi? Explain what you would do.

10. What are name signs? Explain how a person, hearing or Deaf, can get one? From who?

KISS ME
I'M IRISH AND ASL-friendly!

YOU SIGN WRONG!

We don't sign that here!

YOU SIGN DIFFERENT!

EXCUSE ME! "MS. ASL POLICE" ENOUGH!!

BE NICE!

-Gilda Toby Ganezer

ASL POLICE

I have been signing since I was 5 years old. I have been signing throughout all my school years at a Deaf school. I have been signing with my whole family and friends. I have been teaching ASL linguistics at several universities and graduate schools. I have directed and acted in ASL educational films. All this and still sometimes people come to me and say "YOU SIGN WRONG!"...I was like, "Whoa!!!! Excuse me!!" It is disheartening when others, both Deaf and hearing people, try to act like an "ASL Police".

There are many reasons why RESPECT is important. Signers move or travel to a different state because of job transfers, family move, attending conferences, expos or Deaf-related events, vacations, schools, colleges and training.

As a result, signers who relocate brings their ASL skills and dialect with them. Please respect how other people sign due to regional, age, generational and cultural variations. Don't forget signs are affected by various home upbringings and school environments. Don't play "ASL police" with anyone. No one likes that, I promise you. Even if you happen to believe that a sign or a phrase is used incorrectly (either sign production or not matching the true meaning), how you APPROACH is the MOST important thing! BE NICE. The more respectful you are, the more others would feel comfortable with you and return the same respect back to you as well as to others!

If I were you, be open-minded and learn as much sign variations as possible. Like with me, the more you learn, the more ASL-friendly you get. Again, just a reminder, do not play "ASL POLICE" to anyone, period.. ♡Gilda

Discussion Questions

1. What was Gilda's story about? Explain.

2. Where and/or who did Gilda use her ASL with?

3. What does "ASL Police" do? Give examples.

4. Why is it important to respect signers? Explain.

5. What does a signer bring when she/he relocates?

6. What 4 factors affects the way signers sign?

7. Show how you approach a signer signing a word incorrectly.

8. If you are respectful to other signers, how do you think they will feel? What other benefits are there when you are respectful?

9. What happens if you learn all sign variations for a word or a phrase? How will that help you when you travel away from home?

10. If you happen to see someone else acting like an "ASL Police" to a signer, explain how you would educate her/him about it.

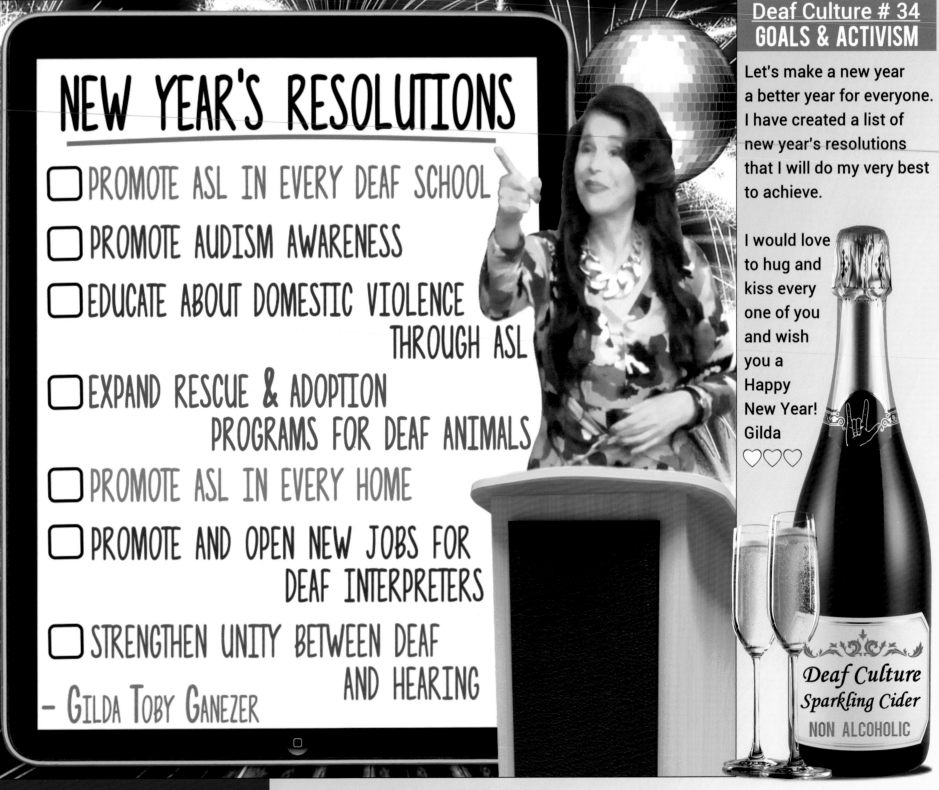

NEW YEAR'S RESOLUTIONS

- ☐ PROMOTE ASL IN EVERY DEAF SCHOOL
- ☐ PROMOTE AUDISM AWARENESS
- ☐ EDUCATE ABOUT DOMESTIC VIOLENCE THROUGH ASL
- ☐ EXPAND RESCUE & ADOPTION PROGRAMS FOR DEAF ANIMALS
- ☐ PROMOTE ASL IN EVERY HOME
- ☐ PROMOTE AND OPEN NEW JOBS FOR DEAF INTERPRETERS
- ☐ STRENGTHEN UNITY BETWEEN DEAF AND HEARING

— GILDA TOBY GANEZER

Let's make a new year a better year for everyone. I have created a list of new year's resolutions that I will do my very best to achieve.

I would love to hug and kiss every one of you and wish you a Happy New Year! Gilda ♡♡♡

Deaf Culture Sparkling Cider
NON ALCOHOLIC

Discussion Questions

1. How do you promote ASL in a Deaf school? Explain.

2. What is Audism and how do you teach others about it?

3. Where can you educate about domestic violence in ASL?

4. What are adoption programs for Deaf animals? Explain.

5. How can you help families use more ASL at home?

6. What is a Deaf interpreter? Why is it an important role?

7. Give 4 ideas on how to strengthen unity between Deaf and hearing.

8. What 2 other new year resolutions or goals would you like to add? Explain why you chose these goals.

9. If you know of a Deaf school that has a communication policy that supports simultaneous communication or "SimCom", what does it mean? How would you feel about it?

10. What was Deaf Protest Now (DPN) about? Explain the history and how it has affected millions of people around the world.

NEW YORK   LONDON   TOKYO   DEAF TIME

DEAF WORLD IS SO SMALL...

WE TEND TO HAVE AN ALL-NIGHT CHAT, ESPECIALLY IN THE KITCHEN!
Well, it's "DEAF TIME"
– GILDA TOBY GANEZER

Why not you people invite me over for just a cup of coffee and some cookies but it has to be in the kitchen so we all can forget about the time and chat all night. Why? Well, obviously because Deaf world is a small one and seeing others sign ASL fluently is something I treasure the most. My neighbors, co-workers, staff, doctors and so many other people near me do NOT sign so who else would I sit down and gossip with? Videophones are really nice but does NOT replace being there in person. Can we do a group selfie over videophone? NO.... Can we do a GROUP SELFIE in person? YES.... The feelings are so different between chatting via videophone and in person. So, as time goes on, news (what's up) and world gossips pile up. By the time when I meet Deaf friends, we tend to sit by the table in the kitchen and chat ALL NIGHT to just CATCH UP like real crazy. That's Deaf Time, which means, no time limit and it ends very, very late. This works the same way at Deaf-related events, parties and many other gatherings where chats would last endlessly!! Isn't that interesting????

Love chatting with you people!

Gilda

Discussion Questions

1. What did Gilda talk about? Explain.

2. Why is it better to meet in person than over a videophone?

3. Why do you think kitchen is a great place to chat?

4. What 3 other locations are also great to meet and chat? Explain.

5. What 4 topics do you think Deaf people like to chat about?

6. What 2 Deaf-related events are popular for the Deaf Community?

7. Why do you think Deaf people tend to chat all night? Explain.

8. Can a hearing ASL signer naturally be part of an all-night chat with Deaf people? Why or why not? Explain your thoughts.

9. What are 3 possible reasons why Deaf people do not or are unable to meet and chat in person?

10. Deaf jokes are one of the things Deaf people love to chat about. What is your favorite Deaf joke? Tell the joke.

USE FACIAL EXPRESSIONS WHENEVER YOU SIGN..

..SOOOO IMPORTANT!!

EYES

EYEBROWS

MOUTH

HEAD

GILDA TOBY GANEZER

In spoken English, vocal intonations are used to help people know if you are asking a question, for example: "What is your name?" - a hearing person would lower her/his voice when asking that question. This works the same way with ASL when we use facial expressions by lowering eyebrows as well as head at the end of the sentence to SHOW that we are asking a question.

Another example - when a hearing person asks, "Do you need money?", she/he would raise the voice when asking that question. In ASL, eyebrows are raised at the end of the sentence to help others know you are asking a question.

So, facial expressions are SOOOOOOO important and a MUSTTTTT when using ASL as a grammatical feature. You make sure to include your mouth, head, eyes and eyebrows whenever you sign. There are NO EXCUSES to be embarrassed to show FACIAL EXPRESSIONS whenever you sign in public! Do not worry about what non-signers think of you because you are doing what you are SUPPOSED to do...Without using facial expressions, we LOSE INFORMATION or could even lead to MISUNDERSTANDING!

Facial expressions are also important whenever using idiomatic expressions, telling stories, giving directions, signing ASL songs, describing nouns and even conveying emotions using ASL.

Here's a tip: wherever you go and sign, be sure to bring your face with you!

Gilda

Discussion Questions

1. What did Gilda talk about? Explain.

2. What did Gilda mean about vocal intonations in English?

3. Explain how facial expressions helps when asking a question.

4. What part of face do you use when signing? Identify all four.

5. What happens if you do not use facial expressions when signing?

6. Tell a short story in ASL. Be sure to use facial expressions.

7. What are the 3 benefits of using facial expressions while signing?

8. Why do you think a signer would be embarrassed to use facial expressions while signing? What is your advice?

9. If you see a hearing person telling a Deaf person not to use too much facial expressions, what do you do?

10. If you overhear a group of hearing people making fun of a Deaf person because s/he uses facial expressions, what do you do?

I have spent my entire life trying to educate others not to view or treat Deaf people like a medical subject. Based on my life, I have learned that being Deaf is NOT a disability...it is a GIFT.

There are COUNTLESS reasons why:

- It is easy to be close with other Deaf people because of how important Deaf Community and Deaf Grassroots (identity, culture, norms, etc.) are to all of us. Deaf people help / support each other EASILY.

- Truly appreciate American Sign Language to communicate and thus to feel connected and CLOSER with others, including Deaf AND especially hearing families, friends, peers and colleagues.

- Can fully UNDERSTAND and ENJOY Deaf jokes, songs, Performances, etc.

- Being Deaf enables us to NOTICE things better (emotions, struggles and even notice things moving around like spirits!, etc.)

The list can go on forever. Again, please throw out that "disabling" attitude. Learn to accept, embrace and appreciate the gifts of being Deaf.

Deaf rocks, always.. Gilda

Discussion Questions

1. What did Gilda talk about? Explain.

2. Why do some people view Deaf people as a medical subject?

3. Explain why it is easy to be close with other Deaf people.

4. How does ASL affect relationships among Deaf and hearing people?

5. What 3 things does being Deaf help with increased perceptions?

6. What happens if a person accepts being Deaf as a gift? Explain.

7. What are Deaf Grassroots? Explain.

8. If you know of a person who thinks that being Deaf is a disability, what would you do about it?

9. If you met a Deaf person who views herself/himself as a disabled person, what would you do? Why or why not?

10. What will happen if the whole family encourages a Deaf relative to realize that being Deaf is gift? What will the consequences be? Explain.

" **DON'T BE SILENT** about things that matter. So, express yourself!!!! will you????? "

— Gilda Toby Ganezer

Visit ©EverydayASL.com

In my experience, SILENCE is definitely NOT golden. Nothing hurts my heart more when I see young Deaf children being unable to EXPRESS themselves in ASL. I was a Deaf child myself, so I know what it was like when I could not say anything to get HELP with. This truly applies to every human being of all ages, THAT'S IT!

Please be kind to share this with anyone you want!!

Thank you, really! Peace and love, Gilda

Discussion Questions

1. Why is silence NOT golden for Deaf children?

2. This issue still happens within families today. Why?

3. This issue also happens within Deaf schools today. Why?

4. If a parent of Deaf child does not use ASL, what do you do?

5. How did attitudes toward ASL change in the past 50 years?

6. What happens if Deaf children CAN express themselves in ASL?

7. How would you feel if a parent wants their Deaf child to ONLY lipread?

8. How would you feel if a parent only wants their Deaf child to communicate using speech. No ASL. What would you do?

9. If a Deaf child does not want to use ASL due to peer pressures or do not want to "disappoint" her/his parents, what do you do about it?

10. Do parents have the right to ask schools to provide ASL interpreters for their Deaf child during the school year? Explain.

LEARN ASL & DEAF CULTURE FROM DEAF PEOPLE'S PERSPECTIVES

There are countless ASL teachers and trainers, both Deaf and hearing, out there teaching the language. As a culturally Deaf person myself who attended Deaf school and interacted / worked / lived with Deaf people since I was 2-years old, I encourage EVERY teacher, especially the hearing ones, to always teach students to also and especially VALUE LEARNING ASL and Deaf Culture from Deaf people's perspectives. Deaf people are your natural teachers that there are so much to learn from them which ASL classes cannot possibly cover.

Go and look for Deaf people as if they are your Easter eggs!

Your ASL teacher and forever friend,
Gilda

Discussion Questions

1. What did Gilda mean? Explain.

2. How does a person learn about Deaf Culture?

3. Can a hearing person understand Deaf Culture? Explain.

4. What does it mean to "think" like a Deaf person?

5. Who is your closest Deaf friend? How did you meet her/him?

6. Do you sometimes prefer having a Deaf ASL teacher? Why or why not?

7. What is ASLTA? Who is it for? Where is it located? Explain.

8. What is the cultural difference between a Deaf school and public school? Explain with several examples.

9. How do some Deaf people feel about hearing person teaching ASL and Deaf Culture? Explain.

10. Like with interpreters, why is it important to be qualifed to teach - not just a person who knows ASL and Deaf Culture. Explain.

Let's have a big party!

EVERY MOVIE MUST BE OPEN CAPTIONED BECAUSE DEAF PEOPLE DESERVE EQUAL TREATMENT!

195432

Gilda Toby Ganezer

I love the movie theater - especially the way popcorn smells, me buying Sno-Caps and Goobers for my cousins, getting so comfy in these big reclining chairs and watching a GREAT movie on a super huge movie screen. Just one more thing I need is a... OPEN CAPTIONED FILM! You know, AUDIOS are added to every film for hearing people and they enjoy. Open captions are our "audio" that helps us understand what the movie is all about. Oh, by the way, foreign films shown in America has English subtitles for everyone to enjoy but when it comes to open captioning for Deaf and Hard of Hearing Americans, it is very hard to get - why???? I was so glad to see that there is a new law that requires theaters to offer movies with open captioning in the state of Hawaii. The state law will end on January 2018; but, someday, a federal law will be passed for open captioning to be available at movie theaters in EVERY state, hopefully! Remember, Deaf and Hard of Hearing people deserve EQUAL TREATMENT. End of discussion!!

Let's share some popcorn, but the root beer is mine!

Gilda

Discussion Questions

1. What is Gilda's goal? Explain.

2. What did Gilda mean about audios in the article? Explain.

3. What is the difference between open and closed captioning?

4. What happens if foreign films do not have subtitles?

5. Explain about the new law in Hawaii about open captioned films.

6. How will open captioning (OC) be beneficial to hearing people?

7. Do other countries offer OC movies for the Deaf? Explain.

8. What do you think about glasses that Deaf and Hard of Hearing people use to watch closed captions at theaters? Explain.

9. What would you do about a hearing person who does NOT want open captioning on films because it is "annoying". Explain.

10. If you want your state to pass a law to require movie theaters to offer open captioned films, what can you do?

IF for any reason I had to speak 1 or 2 words to a hearing person, she or he tries to correct my speech VOLUNTARILY is definitely a big turn-off for me. I am Deaf and I use ASL to communicate, period. However, BECAUSE of peer pressures from society, most of them WANT to look or feel good by voluntarily helping me use speech "correctly" but I don't feel good about it!! Do you know how I feel?? ENTITLED and/or I might say CONTROLLED, no matter if the intent was sincere!! I educate hearing people how imperative it is to be TOLERANT, respectful and NOT to correct Deaf people's speech VOLUNTARILY. I know it is not easy for families, especially, I had a hearing mother who used to try helping me how to speak right and clear... But I was NEVER happy about it and how could I let my mom down? Back then, society used to CONSIDER ASL a TABOO, whoa!! Thank the Lord that as time passed on, ASL became more and more recognized so all my speech training days are absolutely OVER, yes!! I am NOW able to communicate beautifully with ASL and along with an interpreter at workplace, meetings, parties, conferences and more. This is why whenever I had to voice a word or two and then anyone tries to correct my speech voluntarily is definitely not acceptable for me and many other Deafies!!

ASL-definitely, Gilda

Discussion Questions

1. What did Gilda talk about? Explain.

2. Why do some people correct Deaf people's speech voluntarily.

3. How do most Deaf people feel being corrected voluntarily?

4. Explain why it is not easy for some families NOT to correct?

5. How has the attitude towards ASL changed in the past 70 years?

6. When is it okay for anyone to correct a Deaf person's speech?

7. How did ASL become more and more recognized today?

8. If you see a hearing person voluntarily corrects a Deaf person's speech, explain how you would educate the hearing person.

9. If you are an ASL interpreter and a hearing client asks a Deaf client to use speech instead of signing, what would YOU do?

10. If a Deaf person says that she/he is a "failure" because of a poor speech performance, what would you do?

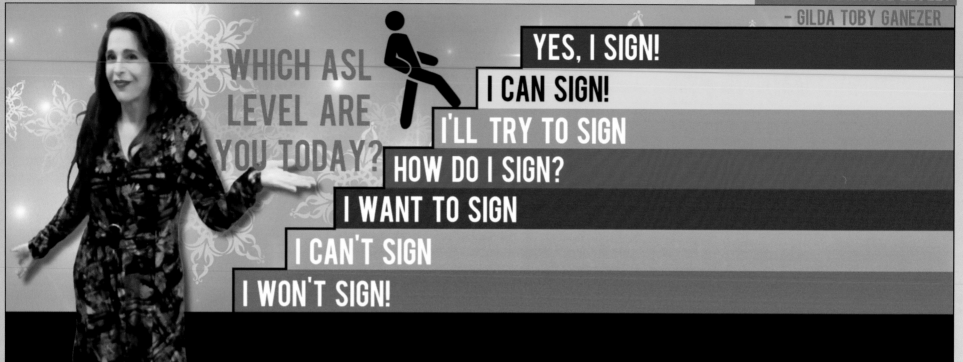

If a person says she or he knows ASL, it really depends on their levels.

What are yours, my dear friends? This picture is about individual's

attitude towards ASL. If any one of you have reached the top level,

let me know and I will give you one real big hug. ♡ Gilda

Discussion Questions

1. Identify all ASL levels seen in the picture.

2. What is your ASL level? What areas do you need to improve?

3. What is an ASL assessment? Explain.

4. What 3 organizations offer ASL workshops and conferences?

5. Where can a person go to get an ASL evaluation?

6. What self-study materials do you recommend that can help with ASL skills? Name several examples.

7. What is the difference between receptive and expressive skills?

8. Which is harder for most people: receptive or expressive skills? Explain your thoughts and experience.

9. Is it okay to ask another signer to repeat some words she/he signed to you? Is it offensive? Is it wise to pretend you understand without asking for repetition? Explain.

10. Which makes a signer more advanced: a knowledge of 10,000 ASL vocabulary words or a knowledge of ASL grammar and sentence structures? Explain.

Time to remind everyone

that Deaf people can do ANYTHING.

Period!  Gilda

DEAF PEOPLE
CAN DO
ANYTHING.
PERIOD!

- GILDA TOBY
GANEZER

Discussion Questions

1. Do you agree that Deaf people can do anything? Explain.

2. Research and explain if Deaf people can become doctors.

3. Can a Deaf person become an astronaut? Explain.

4. Can a Deaf person serve in the army? Explain.

5. Which Deaf person is your role model? Explain.

6. Should co-workers learn ASL because of a Deaf employee? Why or why not? How much ASL should they know? Explain.

7. If a Deaf person was discriminated against in employment, what s/he do about it? What law is going to help with this situation?

8. It's not hard to understand why the President of the United States has one of the most difficult jobs in the world. Can a Deaf person become one? What adjustments will need to be made for it to work?

9. Is an employer required to provide ASL interpreter(s) for a Deaf employee? Why or why not?

10. Can a Deaf person become a police officer? How do you think Deaf AND hearing people would feel? Explain.

CRAB THEORY
STILL HAVE AND NEVER STOPS!

GILDA TOBY GANEZER

I had always thought that as a Deaf person, I would get support from other Deaf people because we share same culture and values...BUT I was wrong.. Whenever I get an opportunity and do better in life, from business to health, some of my Deaf friends would say something negative or worse yet, stab me in the back. I later realized that it is HUMAN nature that cannot be controlled as jealousy and insecurities in others made them want to pull me down whenever I succeed in certain things in life. Just like how you would see crabs pull one another down inside a bucket preventing any one of them to get out and succeed in life. This is a sad reminder that life can be challenging especially when you needed support the most. So, what is my TIP?? Don't be a crab! If you see anyone else do well or tries to do well, give them unlimited encouragement and support, even though if you cannot help but feel these feelings of jealousy or insecurity - which is understandable but when you do not support or encourage others, do not expect the same from them for you in return. Believe me, even strong and successful people do still very, very much need ongoing encouragement and support from others.

This is because you almost always get whatever you give. You would not believe how wonderful it feels when you see others give back to you with support - mutual support will make everyone feel strong and every crab will be out of the bucket and into the sea of success and happiness for life.

One more time to my fellow Deaf, Hard of Hearing, hearing friends and colleagues, DON'T BE A CRAB!, no buts about it.

DISCUSSION CLOSED. Gilda

Discussion Questions

1. What did Gilda mean? Explain.

2. What 2 factors causes Crab Theory?

3. Describe how crabs behave in a bucket.

4. What are Gilda's tips about the problem?

5. What did Gilda explain about strong people?

6. Who are the crabs that you see in the picture?

7. Which word do you think Gilda signed in the picture?

8. Does Crab Theory happens to hearing people from other hearing people, too? Explain.

9. If you see a person pulls another person down with negativity, what would you do about it?

10. If you met a Deaf child who is jealous of a hearing person who could hear music, what would you do to encourage and make that child feel strong? Explain.

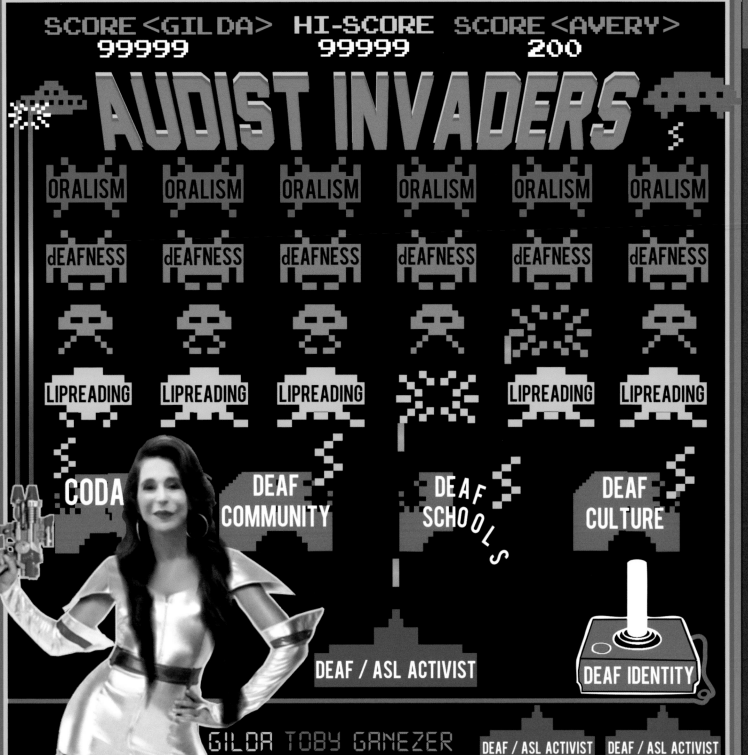

SCORE <GILDA> 99999
HI-SCORE 99999
SCORE <AVERY> 200

AUDIST INVADERS

ORALISM ORALISM ORALISM ORALISM ORALISM ORALISM

dEAFNESS dEAFNESS dEAFNESS dEAFNESS dEAFNESS dEAFNESS

LIPREADING LIPREADING LIPREADING LIPREADING LIPREADING

CODA DEAF COMMUNITY DEAF SCHOOLS DEAF CULTURE

DEAF / ASL ACTIVIST

DEAF IDENTITY

GILDA TOBY GANEZER

DEAF / ASL ACTIVIST DEAF / ASL ACTIVIST

Well.. Audism is everywhere! My aim is to defeat invasion of audism with a laser cannon to earn as many Deaf pride points as possible. People obsessed with oralism, medical deafness and lipreading are being educated by CODAs, people part of the Deaf Community, students / alumni / staff from Deaf Schools, Deaf Culture lovers and even most hearing families / friends. All we need is a team of leaders or I would call Deaf / ASL Activists with a true understanding of Deaf Grassroots / Deaf identity to win this FIGHT!

Kindly do not let anyone take away Deaf person's identity so, every one of you, Deaf, hearing and especially people of young generation, JOIN us to educate others!!

Captain Gilda and Co-Captain Avery

Discussion Questions

1. Describe what you see in the picture.

2. What 3 things are audists obsessed about?

3. What is Deaf Identity? Explain with 2 examples.

4. What is wrong with oralism? Explain some issues.

5. Why do some Deaf people don't like being viewed medically?

6. What can hearing community do to support the Deaf Community?

7. How can social media help strengthen the Deaf Community?

8. In the picture above, Deaf Schools appear to be the first falling apart. Why is that? Explain with an example.

9. Why is it important to educate the younger generation about audism and Deaf people's rights?

10. If you met a doctor who tells families that being deaf is a medical disability and should be "fixed". What would you do?

FOR A SUCCESSFUL DEAF-HEARING RELATIONSHIP, YOU NEED:

TRUST

RESPECT

COMMUNICATION

LOYALTY

COMMITMENT

WOW!

Gilda Toby Ganezer

According to my inspirational quote - it does not matter if a relationship is between:

- HEARING-HEARING

- DEAF-DEAF

- DEAF-HEARING

It is all about the commitment, love, loyalty, trust, respect AND communication that creates successful and long-lasting relationships.

TRUE LOVE KNOWS NO BOUNDARIES FOR EVERYONE!!

Gilda Toby Ganezer

Discussion Questions

1. What did Gilda talk about? Explain.

2. Can a relationship between Deaf and hearing work? Explain.

3. Is Deaf - Deaf relationships the best way? Why or why not.

4. What are the six factors that ensures a successful relationship?

5. Can a relationship with a Deaf partner succeed without ASL? Explain.

6. Which of the six factors do you think is most important? Explain.

7. Which of the six factors do you think is hardest to maintain? Explain.

8. If you are going on a date with a Deaf person, what four places would be best? (i.e.: bowling)

9. If you met a Deaf person who does not want to date a hearing person, how would you feel? Explain.

10. If a Deaf and hearing couple wants to have a baby, what are the chances a child would be born Deaf? Explain.

"I BELIEVE THAT AUDISM CAN BE HEALED WITH AMERICAN SIGN LANGUAGE"

– AVERY POSNER

Let's team up and defeat audism!

American Sign Language is the best tool

in making it happen. Avery

Discussion Questions

1. Do you agree that ASL can overcome audism? Explain.

2. Why is audism still going on today? Explain.

3. How do you think audism has improved since the 1940s?

4. Can a Deaf person still be audist? Explain.

5. How can a Deaf school still practice audism? Explain.

6. Why do most Deaf people dislike the phrase "hearing impaired"? Explain.

7. If you see a hearing person says to a Deaf person, "Oh, I am sorry that you are Deaf." How do you feel?

8. Why do some people feel that Americans with Disabilities Act law does NOT do enough to protect Deaf Americans from employers or companies against acts of audism. Explain.

9. Sometimes an ASL interpreter can be an audist during an assignment. Give two examples.

10. Does audism exist in countries outside the United States? Give several examples of acts of audism throughout the world today.

COMMON SENSE!

I AM WORKING WITH FEMA AND HUD TO PROVIDE

MAJOR HURRICANE WILL HIT THE COAST

LIVE CMN

– YOU <u>CAN</u> SEE THE INTERPRETER

– YOU <u>CAN</u> SEE THE PRESIDENT

– CLOSED CAPTIONS ARE <u>CORRECTLY</u> PLACED & SPELLED

I AM WORKING WITH FEMALES AND HUTS TO (...) PROVIDE TEMPORARY HOUSING ARRAIGNMENTS

MAJOR HURRICANE WILL HIT THE COAST

LIVE CMN

GILDA TOBY GANEZER

– YOU <u>CAN'T</u> SEE THE INTERPRETER

– YOU <u>CAN'T</u> SEE THE PRESIDENT

– CLOSED CAPTION WORDS ARE <u>WRONG</u> AND <u>MISPLACED</u>

Discussion Questions

1. What did Gilda talk about? Explain.

2. What is closed-captioning? Do all TVs have the technology?

3. What is the difference between closed and open captioning?

4. What issues do you see with the illustration above?

5. Why is it beneficial to have an ASL interpreter during news broadcasts?

6. How do you feel if you see an interpreter being cut off during broadcast?

7. Why do Deaf people dislike when captions obscure a person's face?

8. If you overheard person saying that an ASL interpreter on TV is annoying. What do you do?

9. Where would you suggest that closed-captions appear on TV screen? Give 3 examples.

10. If you see that the above listed issues stay unresolved, what can you do about it? Who would you contact?

It is all about common sense!! TV PRODUCERS, captioners and NEWS STATIONS sometimes don't get it. Some of them seem to be closed-minded and anal-retentive when it COMES to ensuring that Deaf Community would understand any news, entertainment and even emergency messages on TV without any visual obscurities ("BLOCKING THE VIEW"). It kills me whenever I see an interpreter being CUT OFF or shown only for a few seconds on TV while the hearing person is still speaking - this "forces" me to read English closed-captions as ASL is my FIRST language that will help me understand the message clearly. Remember, AMERICAN SIGN LANGUAGE is a VISUAL language for most Deaf people. Of course, if there are NO interpreters or ASL performers on TV, then I would accept and appreciate closed or open captionings BUT BUT if an interpreter is on TV, then show it fully, clearly, 100%!

This problem also applies to closed-captioning covering people's faces or wrong words were used by CAPTIONERS. Trust me, I truly appreciate their work and effort, but, I am sorry, seeing people's faces being covered up or noticing how ill-prepared some captioners were prior to the assignment is no different than using non-qualified interpreters at an assignment. Nobody is perfect but, come on, these TV producers, captioners and TV stations should be more receptive to the Deaf and hard of hearing population, no questions about it. Gilda

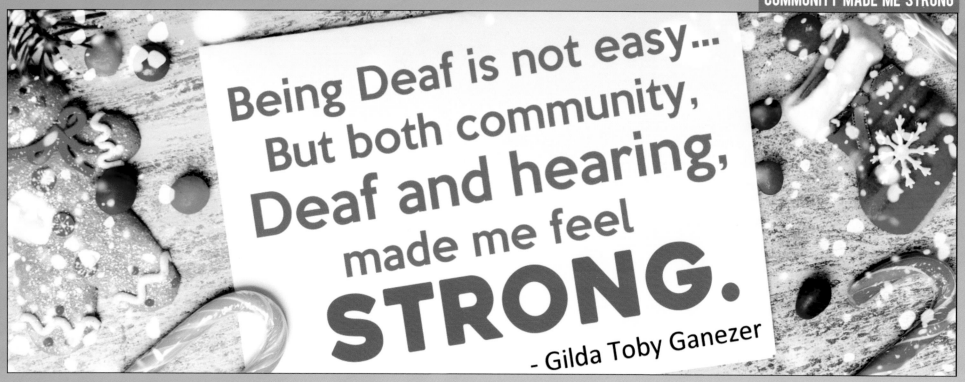

Being Deaf is not easy...
But both community,
Deaf and hearing,
made me feel
STRONG.

- Gilda Toby Ganezer

Discussion Questions

1. What is a Deaf Community? Explain.

2. What did Gilda mean with the quote above? Explain.

3. What benefits do you get by being "strong"? Give an example.

4. What can hearing people do to support the Deaf Community?

5. What 2 events are where BOTH Deaf and hearing people meet?

6. Why do some people capitalize the "D" and the "C" in Deaf Community? What does that mean?

7. What contributions do Deaf people have for the hearing community? Give 2 examples.

8. Name 3 organizations where Deaf and hearing people work together. What are their mission objectives?

9. Why is it important for Deaf and hearing people to work together? What happens if they don't?

10. Is Gallaudet University considered a Deaf Community or a hearing community? Explain your thoughts.

IN 1892, HUDDLE WAS INVENTED BY PAUL D. HUBBARD, A DEAF FOOTBALL PLAYER FROM GALLAUDET UNIVERSITY.

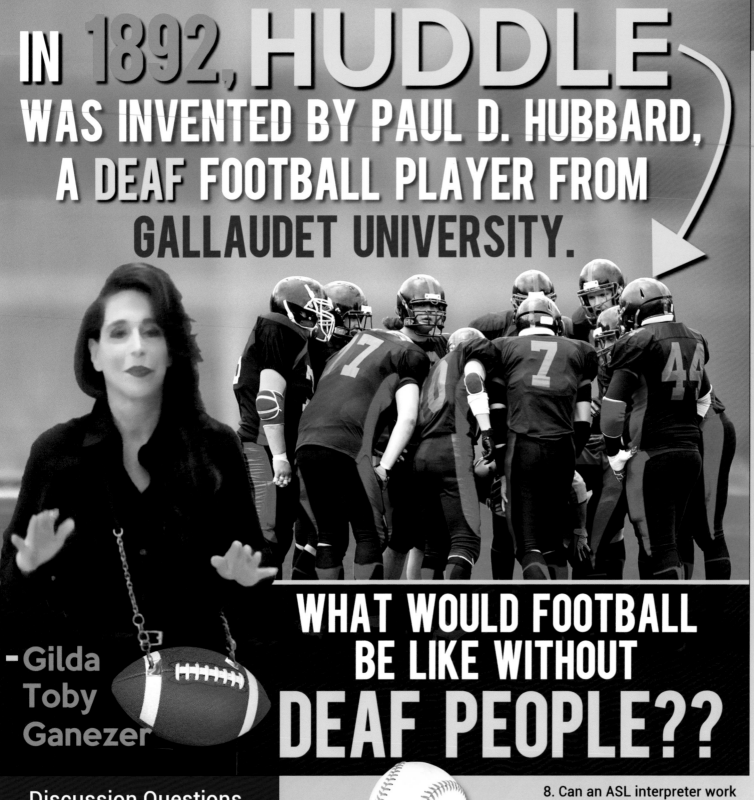

- Gilda Toby Ganezer

WHAT WOULD FOOTBALL BE LIKE WITHOUT DEAF PEOPLE??

Deaf Culture # 50
DEAF & SPORTS

I have watched FOOTBALL GAMES all my life. One thing caught my attention was the way players "huddle" up just before playing. You know what? Huddle was first invented by a Deaf gentleman, Paul D. Hubbard, a Gallaudet University football player in the year of 1892! So, 124 years later, every football team in the country continues to do what they have learned from Deaf people...

This means when you watch the game, you should always be reminded how every Deaf person can make a difference in every part of the world - even OUTSIDE football.

Gilda

Anyway, what do you guys think of my football handbag?

Discussion Questions

1. What did Gilda talk about? Explain.

2. Who was Dummy Hoy? How did he impact on the game of baseball?

3. Name 2 Deaf professional football players. What position did they play?

4. Name 2 more Deaf professional baseball players. What position did they play?

5. What are the Deaflympics? Explain about the event.

6. In Deaf basketball games, how do Deaf players hear whistle blows?

7. What are Asia Pacific Deaf Games? Explain about the event.

8. Can an ASL interpreter work with a Deaf player on the field? Explain how it is being set up.

9. What is so special about Gallaudet University's annual Homecoming event? Explain about the event.

10. Who is Heidi Zimmer? What did she accomplish? Where did she go to make history as a Deaf woman?

This is my 51st quote, through my eyes as a Deaf person. I guess this is because I always see the glass...half full. Hugs, Gilda

Discussion Questions

1. What did Gilda mean? Explain.

2. What is the difference between Deaf and deaf?

3. How do you think a Deaf person would feel being reminded of their hearing disability?

4. If a Deaf child asks you that being deaf is a bad thing in hearing world, how will you respond?

5. Give 3 ideas of what a Deaf child can do to build self-esteem as a Deaf individual?

6. If you overhear negative remarks a hearing person makes about how Deaf people will not succeed in life, what would you do?

7. Name 5 Deaf role models and explain their talents.

8. What kind of alert systems does a Deaf person have at home? Explain how it works.

9. Which children books about Deaf Culture would you recommend for Deaf children? Give 2 examples.

10. If you have a Deaf child, which school would you choose for her / him? Explain your choices.

WHEN YOU INTERPRET, DO NOT LEAVE OUT ANY SOUND EFFECTS.

EVERYDAYASL.COM

©GILDA TOBY GANEZER

Deaf Culture # 52
INTERPRETING SOUND EFFECTS

Sneezing... Blowing my nose...Hiccup...Loud fart... Noisy hunger pangs... Coughing...Clearing throat... Hearing aid whistling... This is HOW Avery sounds every morning... I am encouraging EVERY interpreter to do her/his best to interpret all the sounds in the environment to help Deaf client be aware of natural noises happening. If a hearing person can hear it, why can't Deaf people be given that information, too? So, when you hear a natural noise, from a door slamming to heavy footsteps, be sure Deaf people are aware of them, too.

Please let me give you a kiss (((👄 SMACK))) Psst..interpreter, please interpret that!! _\,,/ Gilda

Discussion Questions

1. Why is it important to interpret sound effects? Explain.

2. Show how you would sign a sound effect of "boom!"

3. Show how you would sign a sound effect of "bang!"

4. Show how you would sign a sound effect of "crash!"

5. Show how you would sign a sound effect of "zap!"

6. Show how you would sign a sound effect of "smack!"

7. Show how you would sign a sound effect of "splash!"

8. What two other sound effects, not seen in the picture above, are important to interpret? Give an example of each.

9. If a Deaf client asks an interpreter NOT to interpret any sound effects, what should the interpreter do? Why?

10. How should an interpreter decide how much sound effects to interpret? How does an interpreter decide what to filter out specific noises? Give an example.

If **A S L** was a snowflake, I WOULD SEND YOU A BLIZZARD.

— Gilda Toby Ganezer

Dear friends,

If any of you are going to be impacted by coming blizzard, you are in my thoughts. Be safe. Stay home from school and work, if possible. At home, you can watch movies, do some ASL jokes, ASL storytelling and/or even make a snowperson with ILY hands.. Think of your pets and be sure they are inside and warm. Stock up some food and bottled water. Stay close to news online and soon this will pass! This artwork is made to encourage you during the storm!

Appreciate your supporting people being affected by the storm,

Gilda

Discussion Questions

1. What is an ASL joke?

2. Tell an ASL joke that includes Deaf Culture.

3. Create an ASL song.

4. Tell a scary ASL story.

5. Tell an ASL story about your ancestors.

6. Show 10 words that uses "S"-handshape in ASL.

7. Show 10 words that uses "L"-handshape in ASL.

8. What should a Deaf family do if their home has a power outage due to bad weather? Explain.

9. Show 15 important weather-related vocabulary words in ASL.

10. What 2 other natural disasters are there? How does a Deaf family prepare for each one of them?

I CAN'T KEEP CALM I'M STILL ~~SIGNING~~ ~~FINGERSPELLING~~ ~~INTERPRETING~~ OH, I GIVE UP!

- Gilda Toby Ganezer

Deaf Culture # 55
ASL OR CHOCOLATE?

I love chocolate more than ASL, really. ...I think.

- Gilda Toby Ganezer

©Everyday ASL Productions, Ltd.

Visit EverydayASL.com

With ASL, you can communicate from:

UNDERWATER

TRAMCARS

AIRPLANES

GLASS ELEVATORS

UNIFORMED FIREFIGHTERS

MOVIE THEATERS

HAZARDOUS MATERIALS REMOVAL WORKER

LIBRARIES

SCHOOL BUSES

THROUGH ANY WINDOWS

SUBWAYS

AND MANY OTHER PLACES!

- GILDA TOBY GANEZER

You don't need a SOUND to communicate!

I celebrate International Women's Day

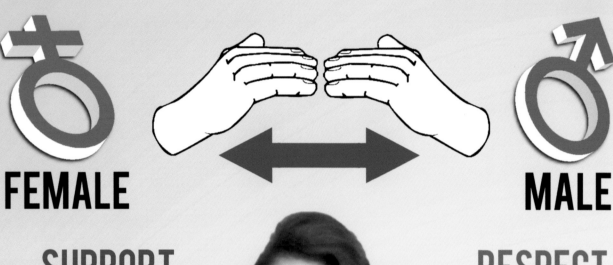

FEMALE

MALE

SUPPORT
DEAF
WOMEN

RESPECT
& VALUE
DIFFERENCE

REMOVE
WORKPLACE
UNFAIRNESS

EQUAL
LEADERSHIP

RECOGNIZE
ACHIEVEMENT
BY WOMEN

MORE
WOMEN
POLITICAL
LEADERS

EQUAL
RIGHTS

EQUAL
PAY

Gilda Toby Ganezer

IF EVERY SOLDIER IN THE WORLD WAS DEAF, THERE WOULD NEVER BE ANY WORLD WARS.

- GILDA TOBY GANEZER